Picking Flowers

by Charles Broderick
illustrated by Dennis Hockerman

Core Decodable 106

McGraw Hill Education

Bothell, WA • Chicago, IL • Columbus, OH • New York, NY

MHEonline.com

Send all inquiries to:
McGraw-Hill Education
8787 Orion Place
Columbus, OH 43240

ISBN: 978-0-02-138064-0
MHID: 0-02-138064-3

Printed in China

6 7 8 9 10 DSS 27 26 25 24 23

Six kids hiked behind Ranger Liz down the trail. The kids liked Ranger Liz.

The kids followed Ranger Liz up high ridges and over wide bridges. They followed her into a field of flowers.

The kids really liked the flowers. Some flowers reached the trail's edge. Some looked like bright spikes.

"I wish I could take some flowers home," said Rick. "They would be nice for my mom."

"Read this," said Mike.

Rick read, "Please do not pick the flowers." Rick looked around the field. It was filled with flowers.

"There are miles of flowers," said Rick.
"Why can't we pick some?"

A yellow and black bee buzzed by.

The bee sniffed at a flower. Rick and the kids jumped back. Then Rick saw a black and yellow finch. The bird sniffed at a flower, too.

"See the bees and the birds," said Ranger Liz. "They need the flowers. And the flowers need them."

Rick was still thinking about his mom.
"But why can't we pick flowers?" he asked.
Ranger Liz smiled.

"Well," said Ranger Liz. "Your mom might like a mix of flowers. You might pick six or seven."

"That's right," said Rick.

"What about your five pals?" asked Liz. "Would they like a mix, too?"

"Yes!" shouted the kids.

"That's a lot of flowers," said Liz. "And hundreds of kids hike here each week. What if all those kids picked flowers?"

Rick was thinking. "There would be no flowers left," he said. "And that would be bad for the bees and birds."

"That's right," said Ranger Liz. "So what do you say now, Rick?"

"Please do not pick the flowers," smiled Rick.